A GRAVE IS GIVEN SUPPER

A Grave Is Given Supper

Mike Soto

DEEP VELLUM PUBLISHING

DALLAS, TEXAS

Deep Vellum Publishing
3000 Commerce St., Dallas, Texas 75226
deepvellum.org · @deepvellum

Deep Vellum is a 501c3 nonprofit literary arts organization
founded in 2013 with the mission to bring
the world into conversation through literature.

Support for this publication has been provided in part by grants from
the National Endowment for the Arts, the Texas Commission on
the Arts, the City of Dallas Office of Arts and Culture's ArtsActivate
program, and the Moody Fund for the Arts:

ISBNs: 978-1-64605-010-9 (paperback) | 978-1-64605-011-6 (ebook)

LIBRARY OF CONGRESS CONTROL NUMBER: 2020932579

Cover art and interior images by Daniel Gonzalez | printgonzalez.com
Interior layout and typesetting by Kirby Gann

Text set in Bembo, a typeface modeled on typefaces cut by Francesco
Griffo for Aldo Manuzio's printing of *De Aetna* in 1495 in Venice.

Printed in the United States of America

CONTENTS

PART I

PART II

○

○

○

PART III

Part I

Blank Chapel or, Consuelo's Mistake

The empty doorway cried escape to her
by name, so she took the invitation
to step in, unwrap the rain from her face

& wait for the storm to pay its sudden visit.
But seeing the vandalized walls, a message

started then smeared, the mad steering
of a hand thru paint—to Consuelo the ruined

whitewash was blindness smeared into sight.
A rage she shouldn't have recognized, the one
house of God she shouldn't have rushed into.

Floors recently laid down, walls primed just
the day before. With the bust of Malverde
set to arrive with the front door

that afternoon. Nothing to stop her from
getting closer, tasting, first with her finger,

the glimmer in the grit. Nobody to keep her
from gliding her tongue across the wall, deciding
salt from the moon—what rushed leaves

& laughter up the ladder of her spine, & no one
with her in the silence after someone cleared
their throat. When, at once, she knew the mud

her bare feet dragged, the shawl she let fall
on the floor, that she would be pulled out
by much more than her hair, turning

to find the faces like a firing squad armed
with blanks, with blame, with stares.

Topito

In the scorched sands outside
of Sumidero, I buried my first toy
& a picture of my mother, said
goodbye to my father who left
determined to get across the wall
commonly known as the brow
of God. After that, the horizon I
gazed at for a grip on what do now,
next, for the rest of my life, gave me
nothing. All I could do was sit,
duck my head into the darkness
of my held knees for what seemed
like hours, enough to fall half-asleep
& dream a section of the wall's shadow
came over & clocked a hat into place
on my head. I woke & looked up,
but the monolith was gone. I stood
& scanned the horizon, spotted
a horse & a rider. That's when I knew
the dream was real. As fast as I could
I ran in their direction. The rider,
a man in a snakeskin vest, slowed
down & told me, *Topito, your hat is all*
black so the brim & the shadow it casts
will always be confused. Now a way
to go unseen is yours, & the inward
journey possible, now you start
seeing how the flesh gets tamed.

Fue El Estado

In the beginning there was murder, & out
of murder shadows & barking ran up
to read ciphers on walls, cold-blooded

creatures plotted their revenge behind
smoke. Under pointy brims names
crossed out from grocery lists, fates

determined by the jeweled hands
of a father who landed his firstborn
into a pair of alligator boots

by the age of five. Birds reassembled
on the first lines between poles after
shots were fired into a Mercury Topaz.

In that silence that's always been the silence
most alive. Mindless bodies, armless minds,
tattooed Marys over scarred wrists,

R.I.P. murals for miles. A shopping cart
full of prayer candles for students not
killed, but handed over, not disappeared,

but missing still. Gossip tangled up with
truth from the start. Turf wars over which
version of time would survive, mothers

bleeding from blown-out windows,
sons deaf now for life. Revenge invented
because justice was not. The first day

a table filled with half-empty cups,
set up to be snatched by streets
of desperate runners even then.

Fog Having Tea with a Graveyard

We caught the tombstones sleeping, or so
we thought. The deeper we walked we knew

the sky had dropped gown to ankles
& the cemetery had company locked in.

Time woven out, minutes into moments,
seconds into the sheer white cloth of a cloud

we now feared to part. The tombs no longer
a shortcut to the other side of town where

water was our mirror for skipping stones.
Even the dismembered statues that became

our trophies—Mary Whose Hand was Swallowed
by Her Heart, Our Lady of the Nose Bitten Off

for Spilling Blossoms from Her Robe—seemed
to conspire with a lust that could exist above

the moss for this morning only. And when
you dared me—*steal the pieces that lay broken*

at the feet of the Headless Angel with a Sword—
that only gave Godspeed to the mischief

already sparked in my mind. But leaving
made that weight come alive on my back,

dragging me down, making me stagger
to the space where the walls crowned

with broken bottle shards paused, & stepped
on the same grave as always to climb out,

but this time barely, with what was starting
to weigh as much as a man on my shoulders.

Ampersand Kings

The stones we skipped, cymbals
struck for every step we walked

them on the water, the ringing trails
& turns we took dedicating throws—

this one for El Mero León Del Oscuro,
& Gusano del Cielo, & Nariz de Estrella,

this one for Conejo Negro, & Chupatierra,
& Chapo the first Topo of drug lords—

& kept tossing until we saw nothing
but silver on the belly of the stream,

until the lack of light became a lack
we unlearned, & we were ampersand

kings, & when one of our throws ramped
the water to reach the other side, the other

side became possible, lit with the eyes
of shadows that started barking

or laughing—we couldn't tell, & always
assumed the golden throw a stolen

piece of our broken angel's head.

Breaking an Open Window

Somewhere in crowds that scowl
in the sun & wait for the procession
to pass, Death is the hired gun who
follows me: a stranger whose stare
is careful: a thief whose patience remains
unhatched, even as tubas thump by
& trumpets seize the air

with a flourish. A criminal disguised
by the sidewalks of people screaming
to get under fists of money thrown
out of SUVs: a teenager pretending
to be impressed by the bust of Malverde,
immaculately decorated on the hood
of a Black Bronco. Side-glancing to see

when I leave: the fat man who manages
to get ahead of me, peel an orange on the corner,
& listen to my keys rattle for the dead
weight of entry while gushing slices
into his crooked teeth: a vendor who
followed me to know the size of the coin
I'll swallow before I step thru

the door. Always a half-second ahead
of me, I catch only shadows of mice
risking the street when I turn, only smoke
waiting to escape my grasp. A question
that won't let me sit down—a trap to lure me

back out when streetlamps kindle & zone
the night, set by the shadow

of a stranger for no reason crossing
to my side of the street. Turning to walk
the other way, I found both—the gift & curse
chasing me into a torn building, up
every flight to have me against the wall.
To hear me break a window with the bone
that begged out of my body.

First Supper

A question happened when I was a boy—a night.
Rows of cups nailed by their handles to a wall, each
one eavesdropping on wind describing the size of maize
outside.

I couldn't escape the table. A dream replaced
the hunger in my stomach, a yearning to be filled
from the bottom up with the wind

of a *Yes*. I couldn't escape
my chair. I had no answer for the table
set with blindfolds

instead of napkins. One woman shifted food
to the side of her mouth that had teeth, a trapped princess
glared, others hissed above the stove. No one
could see me.

Tortillas torn in half over mud, the table
getting satisfied, the gossip getting louder, every plate empty
except mine. I wanted to run, at least to press

my ear against the wall. But only my mother
could ask, *what's wrong?* Everyone's attention
trapped me for an answer. In revenge

I told the truth, *me estoy muriendo de amor.* The table broke
into laughter because I was too young to say a thing like that.

Breve Historia

Consuelo's mother calls her a slug
in a salt storm, writhing on the floor,
sliding thru legs of chairs, their desire
to be set on fire Consuelo felt too clearly
to be called a normal child. Only after
someone hoisted her above their shoulders,
offered her up to the moon, would she
calm down. Her mother disappeared
after the second straight week she refused
to wear shoes. All Consuelo wanted from
the moon, if not a silver dress, at least
a thread to follow. If not a dance with death,
a tunnel connecting her future to a roof full
of rabbits. But anger became a house she
couldn't sleep in, hallways had the voice
of an absence going thru them. Consuelo
lured continuously to the garden where
a birdbath knitted itself to sleep.

Topito's Fate

The wind of that dream lasted a horizon
of years in my stomach, leaving a lone tree

bent in the gesture of listening. That's why
my hand flickered at the dud key of an

accordion in my sleep, why the mood
of that dream took enough steps

into reality, reached the door, & arrived at
breakfast, making my fist a bird too heavy

to fly from the table, tipping over a sunlit
glass of water instead. Those broken pieces

on the floor the coins that bought me
a block of ice, for years the gun frozen

at its center had my name engraved
on its handle.

Consuelo's Vision

Famous—not for walking a fake
distance on his hands, since sleeves
slept empty from his shoulders,

& not for using the cigar stubs
of his legs to waddle like a fish
to his spot. On the sidewalk,

Consuelo sees him, a stump
of a man, surrendered to the void
of his hat, for the glimmer of a coin,

or the feather of a bill. Known
to everyone as an island to leave
undiscovered. Dividing people

in a blur for work, children in
face masks, vendors with
trays of sweetbread balanced

on their heads. Held hostage by his
body, but daring Consuelo to guess
who or what brought him: the need

to send a message, a wheelbarrow,
a vengeful wish granted—with
the cracked mirror of his gaze

which kept healing until she was
close enough to ask him, *Did I?*
If you think his answer was the coin

Consuelo had to swallow she'll say,
no, his smile. Mischievous, a smirk in
the dark, a marble in an empty drawer.

Death the Man Who Silvers the Desert at Night

Practiced my aim, afternoons spent
on the sides of roads, trying to shoot

down the violet pears that sat on pads
of cacti, undamaged. Several rode

intact in my passenger seat the night
someone using a mirror to flash moonlight

gave me the excuse to do in darkness
what the horizon dared me to do

my whole life: pull over, abandon my car,
& walk the distance between the road

& hills. Too far to turn back, the direction
back to my vehicle lost. Just as I resolved

to keep going, a black-clad figure dissolved
out of the dark, tucked a pistol into his belt,

growling *it's a sin to have waited this long*,
but I remember thinking *this is exactly*

my time. As we walked in a circle, I felt
the opposition of magnets between us,

& when I shot snake eyes into his chest,
a sadness rose inside me but not surprise.

I only knew for certain I was seeing
the right signals, taking the right path.

Everyday Tunnels

Explain the road held hostage by
the three-legged waltz of a dog,
twisting milk in his grin—say
it wasn't really a dog, but a man
back for revenge & unable to lure
his adversary out of his home—say
it wasn't really a road, but a dream
our imaginations paved. That's why
our slingshots veered left & we missed
him every time. Explain the day

we ducked supper for the .22 rifle,
became hosts to the noiseless rabbits,
how they arrived like thoughts into
the grass we guarded, & came away
with the bells of three bodies gripped
in our hands, headed to the pines
for a stew on branch-fire, the peppers
Abuelita grew in a wheelbarrow
the secret ingredient. A few spoons

made us mummies trying to talk
our bodies out of going blind,
back & forth wiping our brows
in an ecstatic hell of found time.
Explain, but it won't be enough
for the dice-roll that told us which
rooster to dub with a razor blade,
how it took only a day to train it
to blaze its feathers at turkeys,

even the ones that attacked
Tía when she wore skirts.

So many days are tunnels. At the end
of one, nets of sunlit water for bathing
outside. Another leads to a flea market
where all our money put together
affords only one pair of boxing gloves,
so we flip a bottle cap to decide who
gets to fight with his right hand.

The Dead Women

The killers went to no trouble covering
the bodies, no black plastic bags, no lids

on barrels, knowing vultures would bury
them in a lone cloud. Every day, women

rouse out of sleep, sit up thousands
in the blue-black light to catch

hour-long buses in lots their bodies
know by memory. By early morning

plants hum with the gloved hands
of women assembling screens all kinds

& sizes, LED, LCD, plasma, touch
for smartphones & tablets. Shantytowns

leap into the desert to meet the demand.
At the end of a long week golden arms

dangle out of sport utility vehicles, men
catcall in elaborate necklaces, step out

& tap snakeskin boots to music no one
will tell them is too loud. Women with

their own money might smile, or refuse
in the wrong manner. It's absurd to say

these were not murders of passion, but
the media says the impossible. Imagine

no bars over windows & doors, these
neighborhoods with no layers of graffiti

competing incessantly to stay king. A body
appears along a highway, no one discusses it.

Then a chicken farmer finds seventeen.
It takes a number to shock people now.

You might think a match cannot be struck
on such a suffered surface, no one shouts,

no one snaps, no one has had enough.
Then a mother's heart & mind go blank,

screaming, attacking, accusing everyone in front
of the station, the whole world, of murdering

her youngest, a dancer who had no silicone
implants coroners could use to identify her.

Aluminum children run holding snakeskins up
to every car that passes, shaking them like sleeves
of shirts drivers keep leaving behind.

Out of improvised holes, shanties cooked up
with sticks & soda cans, out of roofs that invent
rags of shade on the ground,

they emerge ecstatic to announce their market:
coyote pup, vulture fledgling, scorpions
clicking in chicken-wire cages raised like lanterns,
like a futile conjure they must attempt

hundreds of times. Hard to know—belt or boot
maker, medicine man—who ever stops to reward
their cunning. On this road only a kettle of vultures
stirs the bored stadium of survival.

But the truth, once in a while, a black
Bronco pulls over, with a rack of ibex
horns as its hood ornament, with dice

that dance from its rearview mirror above
a dash plated with gold, & the eagerness
of those children surrounds the opened door.

They must have a name for the exotic boot
that gravels the ground, maybe God is a man
who comes every thousand cars, lets them
recover their faces in his mirrored sunglasses.

When the firing squad lines up, honey
is what I hear, jars of it glowing
in the sun, the buzzed lasso
of bees hovering above the lids,
a busker's accordion . . .

the vagabond who taught me staring
was impolite takes out his teeth
& smiles. Shipwrecks

of rice, hanging scales weigh clouds
of mulato pepper, a bag of pig's feet—
every sale shakes the dials

from sleep . . . & past a parade of face masks,
the backdoor of the pink corner store
brightens to the scuffed yard where

I set down my first rooster & watch it blaze
its head feathers toward a house of cards.

If I was born into vengeance, dragged
into life to carry death across a battlefield
that doesn't exist. If I was born

into these alleys butchers & vendors use—
drain on the floor, hoses nearby
humming with sandblasts of water—

then the man with a desert scorpion ambered
in his belt buckle has been in charge
this whole time. When I hear another accordion

join the busker, & the men raise up & point,
the scorpion is the one who comes over
to my ear & grins *No,*

that's the sound of Santísima Muerte pulling
her drenched hair out of a bucket.

Mercury Topaz

Trapped in trying, caught in the cloth
of my own dreaming, unable to wish myself
free—somersault snatched in a pelican's gullet,
suffering to wake from a mumbled country
the size of my sleep, with barely enough room
for wanting out. How to know—as the flicker

of a faceless start, unborn, uncoined, desperate
to stay dead (or was it alive?)—why
I was being smuggled in a box surrounded
by the jive of tricksters—whose footsteps
came so crisply after coming to a standstill
the size of an ocean. How to predict

a trunk would fly open, that I would be a man
weeping blindly on a bleached floor
of light, unable to decide if condemned or spared
under the belly of a bridge, as models
of other vehicles sped by. How to ever

bring myself back—to the size of knowing,
who drove, which voices were real.
A few footprints & a coffee left steaming
on the dash of the unlocked car.

Laundry across Balconies or, Deciding to Fold

The jellyfish tethered midair this morning,
floating in the noised vaults between buildings,
sent out sleeping across balconies, were proof

this day arrived under a table of water
to show us its cards. With a high inhuman
kindness, in the wired space where clothes

mean to dry, a voice began but only its solitude
could be made out. Above the snare of sparked
gardens, stray cats sipping a birdbath, a ceremony

of drowned kites hovered, trying to age backward
to the invention of flight. My mind made up
by the birds that flickered away from the wire

while those shirts reeled in the clockwork
of the voice's hands—the first few squeezed
decide that nothing is ready to come in.

Topito's *Yes*

The window cracks open, an ant travels
the sunny side of an egg, & already
the song at my heels is a trumpet
snickering at death, a *Yes*

played simply, resembling a blind
man's cane, or light tapping into
the belly of a knife, flash

that agrees with the countdown
of clicks that crown the bottom
of the black, triggering stove-heat

to rise with the tightly knit noise
of mobs in the street. Demands
for me to give up raising that song
as my child, getting louder;

to declare every minute spent
convincing that flash to be a flame
we could carry, that in turn
would carry us, for at least
a few moments past

the border, into an afterlife of baked
parking lots & payphones, beyond the wall
commonly known as the brow
of God, as a failure.

After hours that could have held water
& didn't, after moments that flickered
like moths but never frenzied the light.

After a day of pouring myself tea
from Death's immaculate silver kettle,
with everyone standing carefully back—
I walked out, the *Yes*

from that morning blazed in my
palm. Held like the last match
in the book, handled like a fledgling
fallen from the branches
of the zeitgeist. Passing

eyes that stopped everything
to accuse me of petty arson, senseless
blasphemy, felony sex. Passing

the supremely unchosen, stares
that stood unlit in doorways,
the incremental wives, with only a few
others that kicked ant piles to join me.

It led us to an altar with a Dance of Death
scene in miniature: tide of skeletons
on emaciated horses galloping toward
small astonished figures of man.

★

By the time it took us to the altar with
the Virgin Mary seated next to Santa Muerte—
arranged as if not caring who sees them

at the same table—we were fifteen
with one flame between us. But down
to just me again at the improvised dock

where that *Yes* was payment, & the sound
of aluminum shadows, empty cans
twisting, signaled the ferryboat coming.

Part II

Sixty-eight were found without heads,
feet, or hands, making the road a land

of taillights, flames for miles blown out
after those of us driving, fed up, abandoned

our minds for the Ferris wheel horizon
above lots & tents. Consuelo woke up

that day to billboards, advertised promises
to dump rival cartels & their families

where their bodies would best decorate
the ground. Sumidero's plaza brimmed

with hissed thoughts & gossip, bitterness
of why & who to blame, flooding

the monument whose folded arms became
pathetically symbolic of the State.

And just as demands to topple the statue
came to a boil, the morgue-bound

procession of those bodies made everyone
step aside & pause. This is how Consuelo

& I met. Of all the drivers who gave up
getting to the other side of their lives

that night, I was the only one dancing
after satisfying a terrible need

to vandalize something in an unfinished
church with a few cans of paint God

must have left sealed for me. Consuelo
the impossible stranger, who took my arm,

told me have respect, but underneath
wanted to know how I could be

celebrating despite those bodies in black
plastic bags making their way thru.

One moment, the vehicle
set on fire at the intersection
is a mirror at the bottom
of the world where we gather

to divine what will remain.
The next moment, it's the reflection
we run away from when the flames
rise & start licking the wires

between poles. One moment,
people in the streets are a river
picking up speed as the sirens
get closer. The next moment,

police lined up with shields
& clubs in their fists are just
another wall to throw rocks at.
I remember sleeves of tear gas

hazing the streets. Consuelo
ducking me under her shawl,
saying we needed to escape
the commotion—how quickly

it came to me where we might
find some privacy & a bird's-eye
view of the drop to a new
low of lawlessness.

At the top of the Ferris wheel, the city
on the other side of the blackout, dressed
in bridges & blinking lights, stared

at our sudden death with an utter lack
of surprise. Windows wide awake

mocked our existence on the wrong side
of the wall. But this moment—stranded
at the apex of the dark, after the veins of all

machinery ran dry, before the panic settled
to dull frustration—when Consuelo seized

my wrist white, told me always in her dreams
an anguished dog yearns to be saved
from the argument it's having with its tail.

This blackout is what it wanted, to be taken
by the scruff, to be stranded in an instant

where the difference between life and death
is a hummingbird. She took my hand into
her dress, told me the difference was smoke,

a snuffed candle's hair. The difference between
black & black if it bled. In between her thighs

the weather was strawberries, the weather
was her rushing to get me inside.

To say I love you put a bird on a wire
so I told her enough times to get an abacus
going in the sky. To follow her body
made my heartbeat a flight of stairs,
of swallows twisting up to the tower
of a bell which went silent on the condition
of Consuelo & me & dusk & the roofs suddenly
everywhere around us. We weren't afraid,
what people thought of us on a distant
ship that would never reach the shore,
& since every day Death said hello in
a different manner, not one kiss went
missing, not one ecstatic gaze, nor
the desire to love each other above
the apathy of passing cars, the people
coming to church, crossing themselves
& us, giving up their blessing by mistake.
The paletero barking out his flavors,
making us laugh, because what kind
of ice cream man is angry.

Looking to get my name written on
a tiny skull, I chose Consuelo's instead.
Paid the vendor with a hole in his hand,

that coin slot bribed barely, but this time
for good. Walked away from his smile,
let the sugar dissolve on my tongue,

& soon enough a town surviving
like a fire at the bottom of an ocean
became a memory of the future:

where a gate keeps the lunatic eyes from trotting down,
where the feast wolves want in the yards is bound to happen,
where the wind that trickles downhill to breeze thru
        plumage is God,
& branches hold the sleeping hens that blink in & out
        of my dreams like devices.

Instructions or, Consuelo's *Yes*

Tear a window on the pomegranate's
flesh, smell the bright blood
of its seeds, rest it on the shoulder

of the grave, let that wound be a light
you left on, place it in the manner
that best punctuates the still life:

gravestone, gray flowers, grade
of moss & lichen grimed over
a three-year Fall. Walk the path

away. Think of the garden you'll inherit
if you turn back, patina on petals, cobweb
branches, foliage veiled with time lost.

Red for the dismantled weight of your thoughts,
red for promises of bloodshed on billboards lit up
      & for once, unkept,
red for the tablecloth snatched out perfectly from
      underneath Death's supper.

Take the memory of that scent, lock it
in a drawer whose key you'll have to
swallow. With you there are moments

sunlight never touches with its fingertips.
With you fire-damp flowers that sway
on a seafloor. With you this need

to arrive at a glowing curtain, enter
the photo booth, & let it give you
a strip of your real face to place
in the corner of your vanity.

The first time I saw Death her dress
was a tripwire. I found a man slumped
under the branches of a huizache, held
hostage by the heat to its shade, his hand
over the wound in his stomach like a lid
that must throttle. He didn't ask for help
or water. He looked up, gave me the lame
bird of his handshake. Whispered for me
to sit down next to him. So I could see
what he was seeing: in the distance a city
underwater, the Skinny Lady severing
a silver thread with her scythe.

A dung beetle climbed out of the dead
man's mouth. He let his last breath sail &
it was the horned kind we used to find
belly up after they battered their bodies
against the wall of our house. Even if you
won't hear me out, I plucked it from his lips,
did what we did back then—leashed its horn
with twine, took it for a walk, & in the end
that was the spark that led me to a tunnel
lit by fluorescent miles of thought, shrines
to Malverde couched into its walls, & an orange
Datsun waiting where an actual road began.

Got out of the Datsun, found myself at
the bottom of a day lit up by the barking
of dogs that appeared on roofs of every
house, tricksters came out of corners selling
hits they called *el rompecielos.* The more
I kept going, the deeper into the noise I got.
A woman showed me the Dance of Death
tattoo on her inner thighs, & I knew I was
in Sumidero. By dusk that was me soaring
upside down, spun in the sky from a pole
wearing the wings of an eagle, & only that
woman with eyes the color black if it bled
could talk me down.

Paloma Negra or, Topito's Mistake

What I remember—getting tapped
on the shoulder, eyes like invitations
to edge the lake, her nakedness
like a moon to my fingertips.

On my tongue, a glowing I could taste. Doors
that opened to the pennies of a field,
getting chased by lightning,

waking with blackened fingernails.
From the footstep my body burned
into grass, I rose & remembered

being told, *this is what you deserve*,
a kiss that spiraled down a stairwell,
dripping in the dark.

That's why Winter
never found me, why I keep a moth
in my wallet, & listen to branches
raking knots out of the wind's hair.

Consuelo Gone

Her eyes were a rifle & I was standing
in the way of the door, & finally when I
moved to let her go, the void she threw
open became a table, an emptiness born
to stand on its head. I ate supper there
every day, with forks & knives that had
to cut nothing into bread, with strays
that crept in to sniff the invention of my
hand, ask what my name was before this
all happened. Death entered, with mud
& rain helpless to ruin the polish on his
boots. With a jug of wine we toasted away
the love my life was not huge enough
to hold. Once he left, leaves & laughter
came in, branches of sound grew around me
like a forest, cicadas built a droning kingdom
with the random throats of toads. Swallows
one after another flew in to cake mud-nests
in my rafters, until cries for worms hatched
everywhere above me, & the only difference
between my pain & the world's pain for me
was the door I could have closed.

One Day a River Won't Stop Leaving My Mouth

Ruined where no hand
could reach me, I tapped
my life on the shoulder,

introduced it to scorched
grass, my past the horizon
I tore myself away from.

I turned myself in, gave up
the names of everyone &
everything I knew. I lost

my trial under neon tents
for generations to come. Guilty
of wanting to whitewash the
billboard cunt of the sky.

Guilty of letting the stations
that stay lit up all night with
second thoughts go to hell
in my rearview mirror.

Guilty of conspiring to find
the tunnel that connects Malverde
to all Topos. That next day

I was ushered to an office whose
only furniture was a chair on fire—
told my sentence would begin

in earnest the moment I got up
from the chair, walked thru

the back door to approach the crowd
outside. Where an absurdist theatre

would come to its climax by breaking
the fourth wall. My new line
of work—be the man burning
when the announcement

to the crowd rings out: *The allegory
of life in the vicinity of death tells us
night & noon coincide in human moments*

*all the time. Scrape the dark dearly
enough, the Skinny Lady will dangle
her jeweled hand out for a kiss!*

Let the rifle sleep & take the path
scuffed by the limping herdsmen,
who threw anger at decades
of cattle to skirt them uphill.

Ask the emerald beetle wallowing
in a mound of shit, the lizard born
to a life of side-glancing, for cues.

Let a line of ants lead you to the hill's
shoulder, where the only clock
is a candle that keeps a picture
of a dead man from flying away.

Marigolds mark the edge where he leapt,

rather than have his obedience at gunpoint
filmed then sent to his family, rather than go
down in his casket with no gold in his smile.

Memorize the candle's prayer:

> It's possible to own what's
> missing, to hear the devil
> grin, & know the meaning
> of pain. It's possible to hold
> what's missing in a cage, to
> know it like the ghost of a
> chandelier, as the swallow
> you think is trapped in the

rafters above you, to keep it
locked in a cabinet whose
key you'll never borrow—
but also it's possible to
let what's missing fly, to
have smoke poured into
the bowl of your hands &
pick up water. To know the
deepest losses end always
with shadows grazing, teeth
tearing sparks from the
steaming ground.

The Wall Commonly Known as the Brow of God

In Sumidero, the wall is always
looming, night & day our North Star,

blunt reminder of the difference between
this life & the one in El Norte. By far

the reason why the ground is gutted with
tunnels, decades of desperate maneuvers,

so many names trapped in trying. If not
a tunnel that connects a pink corner store

basement to the bathroom of a Texaco
where a razor & a change of clothes wait,

then a tunnel that connects a restaurant
table always reserved to the empty pool

of a house in Calexico. If not the tunnel
that takes you to a Malverde shrine

in Agua Prieta said to be teeming with luck,
then a tunnel that runs thru a copper mine

to a greenhouse in Las Cruces. The above-
ground alternatives: snake yourself into

the engine block of a truck, agree to have
your body stacked under cargo, endure

the heat rising exponentially, in a trailer
inching toward the border, with a sea

of other vehicles all in the same limbo.
Covering desert, valley, & mountains.

The wall is an endless mind of steel
bars east of Nogales, creased slabs

in the worst parts of Sumidero, where
many use the barrier as the fourth wall

of their homes. Some sections of the wall
are rigged with ground sensors & tracked

by drones, & some are an open invitation
to walk a cemetery of scorched sand. But

the section stitched into the minds of everyone
that lives here is the section of the wall most

have never seen: miles away where they say
the wall goes into the ocean, & the constant fog

serves to hide that it ends, or to maintain
the awe of it going all the way across.

Death the Man Always in the Pink Corner Store Buying Nothing

Bodies hung from
a bridge, four women,
five men. One by
the ankle, another by
the wrist, the rest
by the obvious.

I stepped forward—
a sound like kazoos
swarmed my head,

lured into looking past
their shoes, trying
to read the messages
carved into torsos.

But shots fired made
me slip death for a silver
moment, forced me
to regain the most
basic composure.

I pulled out my weapon
& wheeled brashly
into the open—

took aim & lucked out
before he did, fired at a man
I had seen plenty of times

at the pink corner store
buying nothing.

The third shot caught
his right hand,
& he just dropped

& sat there, shrinking under
the pointy brim of his hat,
muttering to the bright
wound in his palm.

I brought my shadow over,
began to pace around him
but he never looked up,
just kept muttering

to the lake in his hand.
Maybe he saw a tunnel
at the bottom of it.
I cocked the hammer
back out of respect
& sent him thru it.

Consuelo's Promise

Guilty of ritual vandalism,
of a free spirit's heresy. Guilty
of finding a tunnel that
connected sixty-eight murders

to a fit of ecstasy. Consuelo
ushered into a room, asked
for her name hundreds of times,
sometimes politely, sometimes

with a sneer—told her real name
was *Confundida*, then ordered
to chalk the wall every time
she gets it right. Let out once

the distinction between love
& loss dissolved inside her.
Blindfolded, dropped off
at an intersection with no

choice but to wonder, by
the way people looked
at her—what in the world
they did to her. She put

her head down, kept walking
until she came to the wall,
found a space where someone
rigged a mirror with wire

along with a cup & toothbrush.
Shaken by the face they tried to
give her—half of her hair cut off,
lit up with rage, but already

calming it down to a flame—already
mischief in the promise that might
take the rest of her life to keep.

Missing (Consuelo's List)

The sunlight we caught like water
in our palms, splashing signals to each other
from pocket mirrors—where did it go?

One beat, hello; two beats, I'll be naked
& waiting. The kisses that kept our lips
burning, the night a pair of swings

waited in the weather of a sparkless yard,
the house no one owned or looked at.
Even in the deepest dark the unleashed

laughter, getting home to raise a window
& sleep to wind shampooing the heads
of trees. The sex invented for the occasion

of a lake. When did flames leap into the lap
of those branches, when did neighborhoods
disappear like people inside imposters—

we once knew? Battles worth coming out
alive from, roosters that pecked for seeds
in our footsteps. Now we can't know

what crime made that go missing, what
sleep evened us out. The deer that stared
into our bedrooms dissolved into what

night, answered whose call behind the necks
of trees that never let them come back?
Even nights of recent rain, oil-stain

streets where we watched ourselves walk
upside down for hours. Even in broad daylight
the river of shadows cast down, wings

that swept the daydream away from
our hearts—those birds found a hole
in the sky where? And what about

the flashing scales of fish we once found
startled on the dock—like coins trying
to flip themselves back into water?

The Next Life

The deck of cards we've been afraid
to part for the unlit side of our lives

sits there holding down a table next
to a glass of water the sun might have

poured. The curandero we've put off
visiting for years, refusing the bright

distance between reason & belief,
avoiding the drive from several deserts

away to the noiseless town where he lives,
dreading the house where he'll point out

the pain we've cradled like wet firewood,
where he'll tell us whose jealousy hasn't

let the tall grass sway in our sleep; not
wanting to be in the room where he'll

describe the flower we must steal, tell us
whose picture we must bury in its place

to let the past know it's been uprooted.
But the time comes to rig the Cutlass

Supremes of our fathers, arrive where
every brown-eyed denizen starts giving

us directions before we even say his name.
Time comes to knock on the door,

enter that tunnel when his teenage sons
answer, invite us to sit in the patio

while they fix the stereo of a black Mazda
to the chopped & screwed music we once

hated to the point of love. When the curandero
finally appears, he blots out the imposing

figure we wanted him to be: hoodie sweater,
baseball cap that sends his ears out like a bat.

Smaller & younger & more clean-shaven.
Before we can change our minds we find

ourselves ducked into a room lit by
the deck & the glass of water the sun

could have poured. We sit down, try
to be clever by parting only one card

off the top, but he doesn't even notice,
spreads the cards on the table. The four

we choose when the little man turns
them—windows that let out the wind.

Hourglass with Bat Wings

5.

With boots we've offered
to landmark the sky, tossed up,
caught by the wire as a handcuffed pair

of notes, as bats that would sing
upside down had we not cut out
their tongues to make cradles

4.

for slingshots. Under the barking
of the brightest star, we perfected
ourselves from looking back,

left love like cards of the highest
hand facedown on the table,
& set out—with ambitions to fail

as many times as necessary, find
ourselves barefoot on the other side
of the bribes yellowing the grass

3.

of our youth. Aspirations to be the ones
staggering into the porch-light
of a stranger who would give us

three months' work timbering pine.
We paid a cybercafé attendant with
no face, a pool hustler, a pastel blue

prostitute, finally found the coyote
who led us to the tunnel that connects
a payphone in a field of maize to

a parking lot surrounded by desert
in every direction. By walking
three days under the clean stare

2.

of a sun we took to be shining
upside down, by finding mirrors
of water we could never drink.

By selling the best years of our lives
to Death, who turned them into a pair
of songs on the jukebox, we got

1.

the desperate money we needed, paid
the best lookout along the wall—
a twelve-year-old with the hair

of a caterpillar—who knew when shifts
ended, which agents liked to nap.

Part III

The sadness of a fully dressed man walking underwater. Denizen of a fountain, a bottom where voices are heard long after their wavering faces withdraw. Watching people's wishes flutter down to my palm, while pinning heartbreak, severed flight, & midair murder, on Consuelo, a rifle hidden in her summer dress—& the witnesses who claimed she knew no better might be the same thieves who noticed my insignificant splash & dragged me out of the water for the coins in my fists— then left me at the door of a curandera who kept an orphanage for animals that refuse the bit. She pulled out a piece of smoke, tied it to my belt loop. *Now walk into no doors & under no shade. Come back after the Litany of Saints.* None of which made sense to a heart not done with falling. But when I returned Consuelo waited on top of a brown horse, & the pattern on its back I read as the white of an old world, so many crashed moths. *The saddle is brief,* the curandera told me, *get on behind her.* We climbed up to the faces of rocks exhausted by the crossing out of names. The roofs quietly below us—when something entirely not her, not me, agreed to the gallop that poured us down, over jagged stairs of rock, buzzing shrubs, past every wire held by the thoughts of trees. Given over, flying down, taken before yes or no intervene. For the first few

seconds after I swore, not weight, not steam,
not the mute wild hair of a comet—that what
I felt leaving was not from us at all. Nor from
the horse catching its breath in one color.

Consuelo's Shawl

The shawl Consuelo lost
was turquoise, green if gray
was caught dreaming.

Heirloom knitted
by the spidery hands
of her grandmother,
let go of by degrees
as Consuelo memorized
the lives of the saints.

When marks charting
her progress covered the wall,
her abuela wiped it clean,
sat Consuelo down, & taught
her the pattern so she could
finish the final portion.

From then on that shawl
was a shield she could always
wrap around her head.

The Invention or, Consuelo's Explanation of the Third Eye

A man swallows a mirror & thinks death is certain,
but it isn't. The mirror goes on reflecting until it becomes
a satellite of sorts, relaying images to a screen sitting secret-
ly in the caves of his mind: internal organs blowing like
pipes in mud, the curtains of his blood, flowing—even the
tremors of his hunger are visible.

He imagines a life tormented by insight, the mirror's
edges sharp against his bowels, but the pain shrinks to
a mere discomfort, & after years he even grows creative
with the mirror, & learns to see a furniture of disharmony
thought to have no apparent form: a pendulum rigged
against its own gravity, a tennis match at the heart of a
labyrinth generating its branches.

Once in a while, the mirror is stunned into bright-
ness, but he never recovers from the glare in time to find
the initial light. He thinks telling this story will make him
famous, but not even his closest friends are impressed.

Finally, he gives up the idea of ever getting it out
& resolves to use the mirror to some unseen advantage,
thinks maybe he's swallowed a system for grounding the
illusions of his mind.

Dressing up a Drug Lord

To wake & wind up standing
in the same room, hands held together
formed a locket for his picture,
side by side facing the corpse
that loomed, washed & famous,
on the table. To know,

by the pair of coins & the pile
of marigolds, the Sunday clothes
& comb glowing atop the orange tin,
we were locked in with an obvious order.

Cornucopia in a coffin: garlands,
lacquered crosses, the spur-blade
of a rooster, pomegranates still ripening,
bottles of añejo— the ecstatic kind.

Everything needed to improvise
Consuelo's first time & mine: sheers
& shapers, shadow-kits & tweezers,
beetle-theatres of jewelry.

Many would say, *too young*,
but we knew sand as the sound
of trying to feed a dead man's arms
to his sleeves, so we used the scissors
to bottom out his clothes.

Consuelo wrapped the tie around
her neck first, imagined his preference.
I walked every button

thru its eyelet, like a waiter
carrying a platter up
to the last flight, where we closed
the wings of his collar & served
the freshly minted knot
to his Adam's apple.

By then we knew: laying one coin
heads & the other tails on the scales
of his eyelids would keep them bribed,
thru the darkness, between the thighs
of Death forever watching
supper arrive on her table.

Hundreds of hired mourners outside, restless
trombones & shovels, pallbearers pacing,
& what must be his widow beside
the flügelhorns. Mother with her granddaughters
probably, tired of the sun—ex-lovers
in their blacks.

Flowers tucked like dawn around
his shoulders, lapis rosary lighting
the fingers of his left hand, & cradled under
his right arm—gold-plated cuerno de chivo.

Only then did we feel bold enough
to knock from the inside out & lie:
we were happy with our work
& yes we were done.

Paloma Negra

Those eyes the color black if it bled
were on us. I could feel the negative
star of her stare from the corner table
where she sat by herself in an aura
of dense gloom. Consuelo locked
eyes with her over my shoulder,
wondered aloud if she was ever
going to leave us alone. Bitter pull,
bitter tide—we resolved to ignore her.
To my astonishment she fired at me
while my back was turned. The bullet
exited thru my stomach, stained my
hand when I tried to catch the pain.
My own blood made the handle too
slippery when I reached for revenge.
When I managed to turn around Consuelo
was nowhere to be found. I had the entire
room to myself. The silence was alive
& emptiness roared. Dimming fast as I
made my way to the door, I walked out
to the astonished crowd in the street,
managed to catch that woman grinning
into the passenger seat of a Grand Marquis
with a charm of crow feathers glimmering
from the rearview mirror & what had
to be Consuelo at the wheel.

Square inside a Circle

Ages ago, this ring
was a ring for bulls,
built with stone, brought
in wheelbarrows,

by minds who thought
Sumidero would always
be a family town, not a city
engulfed in violence:

3,766 murders this year
not counting the unfound,
missing, or disappeared.

Today a much younger
crowd comes to watch
the men who bang rolls
of money out of their
shirt pockets, place
bets on the grass.

Sometimes while getting
the spur-blade tied to the back
of its leg, a gallo will mistake

dusk for dawn & let out a crow
in the middle of the commotion.
People scream: *Ya ven! Órale
cabrones, aflojen el dinero!*

Golden arms, boots of exotic
leather, several which point
like prows of ships.

When they square off
the roosters like two
sparks trying to get out
of the same box.

Death the Greedy Politician

They said it couldn't be done, but I
tunneled a path between a toolshed
& the private residence of his golf resort,

made my way clean thru the manicured
hills in the dark, came to the rectangular
glow of his swimming pool, said a brief

prayer as I stood at the edge of the emerald
water. Thru the glass doors I could
see him at his leisure—on the couch,

belly out, drink in hand, television screen
bathing him on & off in swaths of light.
The volume turned up loud enough, I

opened the doors unnoticed, & before
he knew it, the corner of his eye was mine,
I made a few greasy lifetimes flash before

he could even realize he was trapped.
With my pistol I motioned for him to
get dressed, get ready. When I walked

him thru the brightness of his front door
it was dawn, a crowd had assembled on
the grass, & one of his minions emerged

with his gun on an embroidered pillow
as usual. I stared him down, felt the live-
wire confidence, felt keen & done with

thinking it thru. When I turned my back
to walk the proper distance, I felt him
take the bait, dropped to a knee,

hooked my pistol under my left arm,
& fired. I took his shoulder off.
He couldn't raise his arm. Everyone

jeered & thought it was over, but it
wasn't. He ordered one his minions
to shoot me. He refused. He ordered

another—he didn't budge. I stepped
toward him, shot the wig off of his head
like you might blow out a candle—

indiscreetly & without thinking twice.
When he started running, I put a shot
in his culo. Even though it was a crisp

morning I clocked his humiliation along
with his astonishment at high noon.
I told him to stand up, I made him strip.

I shot his manhood off to make the
cipher complete. I knew it would
make sense once I did it, but not

what kind of sense. The silence
was alive as it's ever been. When
the only clouds left in the sky

merged with an enormous implied
shattering—& for so many days after—
I found myself trapped in a tower

I eventually climbed out of only
to find myself trapped even further
by the desert in every direction.

The Useful Rituals

Before, in sleep, we've put our hands
together & called a distant warmth
to come halo our feet when the sheets

have been thrown from our bodies,
summoned that sensation to rise from
our toes to hover above our heads

like a hummingbird. And when we
wake up our hair is perfectly combed
& parted, steaming as if our dreams

had us working in the cold. And because
we've slept the entire day in order
to be awake the entire night,

we enter the cemetery with the sun
gone down, gather our first thoughts
with a cup of black as the first wreaths

arrive. Two men each carry the golden
weight of flowers caked so densely
to the door-like frames. And since

there's always some pendejo trying
to do it all by himself, we lend our
shoulders & learn two versions

of the cross sit on top of each other
because the useful rituals survive,
learn moths flicker above the graves

because the men decorating the entrance
with marigolds have decided for the third
time the arch needs more. When it's night

enough the ether that dances above
the flames can be seen. Some may never
notice, or it might come to them all at once,

when enough families trickle in, start dressing
the tombs of loved ones—the labyrinth
everyone must walk to avoid stepping on

the graves of others. A mother hands a spade
to her daughter, straightens the picture
of her husband after kissing it several times.

There is a feeling to take away when the cemetery
is lit up like this, hands shaking like cities
in our pockets because it's gotten cold—remember

completely enough, notice the seeds already
held in your fists, the ones that will lift our lives
above the ground just the inch we need.

Untitled (Tunnel with Horse & Rider)

That night told my life, *be a tunnel, connect*
the gold-green wind to the breath you'll use
to clear the dust caked on Malverde's shrine.

To reach the unlit side of my life I became
a prodigy, suffering to wake from a dream
twice the size of my sleep even then, when

people said a curse, a weight that doubled
at night, that Death disguised as dreaming,
sat on my chest while I slept. But I only felt

misunderstood. When I overheard a rumor
the first ever shrine to Malverde lay hidden
in plain sight in a used car lot somewhere

in Sumidero, I took it as a life & death matter
to see the unseen. After years of wandering
lots of old Beetles, Buick LeSabres, luxury

Broncos, getting kicked out of dealerships
for being bearded & weird. After leaping
waves of barbwire on walls at night,

a dash covered in banana leaves called
to me by name. I opened the door
to a late-model Astro hollowed out

to house the stones that first made
his grave. Above them, a cornucopia
slept around the vague bust of Malverde.

Finally, with my chance, I took the deepest
breath I owned, blew the veil from his face—
& when I placed my hat on his head,

the trembling I carried for years inside me
paused like a deer from drinking water;
& in the nondistance between us, awoke

a neon quiet where I dumped all the marigolds
of all the cemeteries I've seen, lit the candles
I didn't bring, & poured him the añejo

I could never afford. A space where I could
sign my name with my knees & ask for help.
I knew the next phase of my life would need

a different tunnel: one that connected
my ignorance to an isthmus where I am
a rider letting his horse graze the grass.

Topito's Poise

To mute the blood, enter the room
with the neon labyrinth, to lay
my weapon down by its entrance,

walk the spiraled path
as a string of silver memories
gets brighter in my mind:

my grandfather braiding a sling,
my grandmother tearing tortillas
into a bowl of milk, & the cats
coming out of nowhere . . .

To stand over the trapdoor
at the heart of the labyrinth,
open it, & find a second spiral
in the stairwell.

To set foot on a ground
teeming with light, pull out
the .38 hidden in my jacket,
cock the hammer back,
& approach deliberately.

To sense the crow perched
on the table understands
why I've come. And when

it flies into the darkness of
an empty doorway, a man
in a snakeskin vest emerges,

& when he asks why the hat
he gave me isn't on my head,
that space wobbles like a red
comb on a black rooster, &

when I tell him I placed it on
Malverde's head, his smile is
all silver, his hand holds out
a lizard that has shed its tail.

Consuelo in the Poppy Fields

Sparked on the steep terrain of a town just west of
Sumidero—fields of poppies where lentils once thrived.
Some still remember the black smoke, how quickly after
the men with torches in their hands & bandanas over their
noses left, the ultraviolet flowers blanketed the hillsides.

The most lucrative drug market the world has ever
known raged into existence just north of the border. The
cartels responded to the soaring demand with exponential
growth. One field became seven. Experienced workers be-
came supervisors, putting the word out, posting flyers for
people built low to the ground. Teenagers poised enough
to come on as security transformed the fortune of their
families instantly after generations of humble earnings. The
vow never to return to a life of having nothing always a
live wire.

During collecting season, a full moon on a clear night
might bathe the fields in the pull of a light that makes
milk from the scored pods come. Consuelo grew up here,
claims on such occasions hummingbirds of a nocturnal
breed arrive & become ecstatic from sucking on the pods
left oozing, slow down from their hyperawareness to perch
on the rocks in their delirium. The iridescence of their
feathers a green rarely seen.

A Few Visions (Topito's List)

Sometimes there is a table at
the heart of a labyrinth, with
a cross made from kernels of
maize beneath it, & a supper I
must get to before it gets cold.

Other times, the heart holds
a chair caught in a dream-fire,
& the labyrinth is lit up like
a circuit. A path so obvious
it tames me to a core of
forward motion.

To sit down willingly, learn
to breathe, thru the rising
flames see the ship that sits
under the stars like a mountain
waiting to be unmoored,

to grasp the poise of dragonflies,
hummingbirds, deer—all creatures
whose complete stillness is ecstatic.

To know the day after death I'll
walk thru an empty doorway,
find myself in a field of moonlit

grass, I'll roam a black & white
world where intuition sees more
than sight & sight is not susceptible

to all the pretty lies. The day after
death I'll find Consuelo on the tips
of her toes, trying to glimpse into
a flickering window. Even now
I'm dying to cradle her foot
in my hand & buy her a look.

Malverde Chapel or, Consuelo's Revenge

Gratitude inscribed in gold,
carefully thought out dedications
on plaques for cargo passed safely
across the border. Black hats stuffed
with dollars, copies of recently
obtained deeds & passports.

Some arrive in monster trucks,
others in vintage cars with airbrushed
murals on their hoods paying homage.

Those who believe more & more people
seek Malverde's help for distorted
reasons say nothing. Don't say anything
about the vendors selling keychains,
Malverde wallets, the rows of plastic busts.

Consuelo skirts thru the crowd,
moves in like a cloud over the day
to darken it. She recognizes the faces:

the man with a flattop in a black
leather jacket, the one with the face
of an iguana, the other wearing
mirrored sunglasses had a diamond grill
that read CHANGO when he smiled

at her. Consuelo gets close to the man
with the flattop. For a moment he stares
right at her, but can't place who
she is. Consuelo holds her hand out,

shows him a prickly pear split down
the middle, its ultraviolet redness
irresistible. He can't help but reach

for it & shock his hand with spines.
By the time he looks up, his eyes
are yellow, the room is lit with
faces trying not to look,

& Consuelo is in the street thinking
how much better the chapel looked
hollowed out, the bright hum of its
emptiness, the ecstasy of landing

in front of those walls, pushed by
a storm into that space Topito
had smeared—the delirium.

Memento Mori in Three Exponential Ifs

1

If every star is a grave, I've held tunnels
against the windows of trains when they
mirror the face of me trying to look out.

2

If letting go is a kind of light, I've floated
candlelit ferries away from my fingertips,

watched them invade my dreams to stretch
the vanishing point back a few miles.

If letting go is a kind of light, the live handles
of a kettle once burned me, blackened

copper was once the night, & afterward,
until the day they unwrapped the bandages

from my hands, I slept backward—awake
in my dreams, asleep in the so-called real.

If letting go is a kind of light, I've set fire
to mansions, memories no longer

tracks to follow, every picture a horse on
the ground writhing from black to burned.

3

If the Dance of Death means love has lured me
into a black Lincoln whose body has been polished
to ring the entire road back, then I've deflowered

the muse in the back seat, bribed the black gloves
of a driver to go around the block a few times
before arriving to the porchlight of a house

I always knew was mine. If the Dance of Death is
the pope, president, pink corner store prostitute,
two-stepping to the same song played backward

& slowed down; if the Dance of Death is a square
inside a circle no one escapes, some play by rules
& die with regrets, others say fuck rules & die

astonished—I've let a skeleton with a third eye
take me by the wrist, I've danced in Death's
strobe light with hundreds of others who needed

to unwind. If the Dance of Death means I've been
saying *Yes* to the same Skinny Lady in the silver dress
that has made her lucky for thousands of years—

I'll weigh my heart against a feather at the scales
& win. I'll greet the end with the swagger
in my heart jeweled & intact. I'll hold hands

with the factory worker, the woman who
Hula-Hoops at the light for money. If the Dance
of Death means I'll use my last *Yes* to leap

the space between reason & belief—I'll fly
out of this life as only a swallow trapped
in the rafters can. If I step thru my front door

& find no floor to speak of I'll sing *Cielito Lindo*
all the way down. I'll tell the skeletons holding
my hands it was me who turned over all

the tables & laughed maniacally in Death's
banquet hall. If the Dance of Death
descends on the distracted

faces of man—I'll be fine, this whole time
I've been a wrestler who entered the ring
only to have his mask taken off,

so I could be naked, humiliated, robbed of all
sarcasm—so I could finally put down the gun
& pick up the fight. If the Dance of Death

represents the courtship between matador
& minotaur, if the allegory means none of the stars
are graves & letting go is not a kind of light.

Death the Coppersmith

Death stared at me like I was one
of those clocks with a bird in its belly.
I turned my back on his handshake
to run but a gun on a table blocked
the way out. I knew the game had
changed. A prayer lit immediately
on my lips:

> Malverde, tú que
> moras en la gloria y
> estás muy cerca de
> Dios, concédeme este
> pequeño favor: llena
> mi alma de gozo,
> dame reposo, dame
> bienestar, y en los
> espacios más oscuros,
> hazme dichoso.

The note next to the gun read:
> Eres el rey—Consuelo,

in her handwriting but her hand
was forced, you could tell.

Pearl handle, silver fixtures, my first
& last name engraved on its handle.

Outside, the bright grind of our footsteps
signed our fates to the showdown.

It's true the tiny hourglass that stood
between us told us when to draw.

It's true the hole I made of his left eye
with my first shot was the only one I got.

I fired over and over but my hand
veered left to miss him every time.

All the holes he put in me, one
after the other, leaked with my

life & the last thing I remember:
Death with one eye coming

toward me, the copper kettle he
carried turning black then green.

ACKNOWLEDGMENTS

Thank you to the editors of the following publications where many of these poems first appeared:

The Arkansas International: "The Dead Women"
Birdfeast: "Everyday Tunnels"
The Boiler: "Paloma Negra or, Consuelo's Mistake"; "Fue El Estado"
The Carolina Quarterly: "[Let the rifle sleep & take the path]"
The Cincinnati Review: "Dressing up a Drug Lord"
fields: "Instructions or, Consuelo's Yes"
Fou Magazine: "The Invention or, Consuelo's Explanation of the Third Eye"; "Laundry across Balconies or, Deciding to Fold"
Fugue: "Mercury Topaz"
Gulf Coast: "[To say I love you put a bird on a wire]"
Hobart: "[Aluminum children run holding snakeskins up]"; "Topito's Fate"
Hot Metal Bridge: "Breve Historia"
Huizache: "Breaking an Open Window"
Interrupture: "Consuelo's Vision"
The Iowa Review: "[The first time I saw Death her dress]"; "[A dung beetle climbed out of the dead]"; "[Got out of the Datsun, found myself]"
The Journal: "Death the Coppersmith"
Michigan Quarterly Review: "[At the top of the Ferris wheel, the city]"
Moonstone: "[Looking to get my name written on]" "Ampersand Kings"
New Delta Review: "First Supper"

PANK: "[Sixty-eight were found without heads]";
"Missing (Consuelo's List)"; "Blank Chapel or,
Consuelo's Mistake*"

Rust + Moth: "Fog Having Tea with a Graveyard"

Poetry Northwest: "Hourglass with Bat Wings"; "The
Useful Rituals"; "Topito"

Radar Poetry: "[When the firing squad lined up, honey]"

Shenandoah: "The Next Life"; "Consuelo Gone"

Thank you to Maria Chelko and Claudia Cortese, whose
close reading helped shape many of these poems. A special
thanks to Kelsey Shwetz, whose insights helped me finish
this book.

Thank you for the love, support, & comradery that helped
pave this book's path: Diego Enrique Flores, William G.
Lockwood, Rebecca Satellite, Lux Ruiz, Martha Elena
Eyzaguirre Ordóñez, Anna Stockwell (for the Useful
Rituals), Sophia Sunseri, Boris Tsessarsky, Joe Milazzo.
Thank you to Vermont Studio Center, and my peers of VSC
April '19. Thank you to my peers & teachers of the MFA
program at Sarah Lawrence College. Thank you to Suzanne
Gardinier for reading this manuscript's cards.

Many thanks to Will Evans for his faith in this book, & to
my family for their love & support.

In memory of Nevada Hill & Thomas Lux.

MIKE SOTO is a first generation Mexican American, raised in East Dallas and in a small town in Michoacán. He is the author of the chapbooks *Beyond the Shadow's Ink* and, most recently, *Dallas Spleen*. He received his MFA from Sarah Lawrence College, & was awarded the James Merrill Poetry Fellowship by Vermont Studio Center in 2019. *A Grave Is Given Supper* is his debut collection of poetry.

PARTNERS

ADDITIONAL DONORS, CONT'D

Erin Kubatzky
Ester & Matt Harrison
Grace Kenney
Hillary Richards
JJ Italiano
Jeremy Hughes
John Darnielle
Julie Janicke Muhsmann
Kelly Falconer
Kevin Richardson
Laura Thomson
Lea Courington
Leigh Ann Pike
Lowell Frye
Maaza Mengiste
Mark Haber
Mary Cline

Maynard Thomson
Michael Reklis
Mike Soto
Mokhtar Ramadan
Nikki & Dennis Gibson
Patrick Kukucka
Patrick Kutcher
Rev. Elizabeth & Neil Moseley
Richard Meyer
Sherry Perry
Sydneyann Binion
Stephen Harding
Stephen Williamson
Susan Carp
Theater Jones
Tim Perttula
Tony Thomson

SUBSCRIBERS

Audrey Golosky
Ben Fountain
Ben Nichols
Carol Trimmer
Caroline West
Charles Dee Mitchell
Charlie Wilcox
Chris Mullikin
Chris Sweet
Courtney Sheedy
Dan Pope
Daniel Kushner
Derek Maine
Fred Griffin
Heath Dollar
Hillary Richards
Ian Robinson
Jason Linden
Jody Sims
Joe Milazzo
John Winkelman

Kate Ivey
Kenneth McClain
Kirsten Hanson
Lance Stack
Lisa Balabanlilar
Luke Bassett
Margaret Terwey
Martha Gifford
Megan Coker
Michael Binkley
Michael Elliott
Michael Lighty
Molly Lunn
Nathan Dize
Neal Chuang
Radhika Sharma
Shelby Vincent
Stephanie Barr
Ted Goff
Vincent Granata
William Pate

AVAILABLE NOW FROM DEEP VELLUM

FORTHCOMING FROM DEEP VELLUM

AMANG · *Raised by Wolves*
translated by Steve Bradbury · TAIWAN

MARIO BELLATIN · *Mrs. Murakami's Garden*
translated by Heather Cleary · MEXICO

MAGDA CARNECI · *FEM*
translated by Sean Cotter · ROMANIA

MIRCEA CĂRTĂRESCU · *Solenoid*
translated by Sean Cotter · ROMANIA

MATHILDE CLARK · *Lone Star*
translated by Martin Aitken · DENMARK

LOGEN CURE · *Welcome to Midland: Poems* · USA

PETER DIMOCK · *Daybook from Sheep Meadow* · USA

CLAUDIA ULLOA DONOSO · *Little Bird*, translated by Lily Meyer · PERU/NORWAY

LEYLÂ ERBIL · *A Strange Woman*
translated by Nermin Menemencioğlu · TURKEY

ROSS FARRAR · *Ross Sings Cheree & the Animated Dark: Poems* · USA

FERNANDA GARCIA LAU · *Out of the Cage*
translated by Will Vanderhyden · ARGENTINA

ANNE GARRÉTA · *In/concrete*
translated by Emma Ramadan · FRANCE

GOETHE · *Faust*
translated by Zsuzsanna Ozsváth and Frederick Turner · GERMANY

PERGENTINO JOSÉ · *Red Ants: Stories*
translated by Tom Bunstead and the author · MEXICO

JUNG YOUNG MOON · *Arriving in a Thick Fog*
translated by Mah Eunji and Jeffrey Karvonen · SOUTH KOREA

TAISIA KITAISKAIA · *The Nightgown & Other Poems* · USA

DMITRY LIPSKEROV · *The Tool and the Butterflies*
translated by Reilly Costigan-Humes & Isaac Stackhouse Wheeler · RUSSIA

FISTON MWANZA MUJILA · *The Villain's Dance*, translated by Roland Glasser · DEMOCRATIC
REPUBLIC OF CONGO

GORAN PETROVIĆ · *At the Lucky Hand, aka The Sixty-Nine Drawers*
translated by Peter Agnone · SERBIA

LUDMILLA PETRUSHEVSKAYA · *Kidnapped: A History of Crimes*, translated by Marian Schwartz ·
The New Adventures of Helen: Magical Tales, translated by Jane Bugaeva · RUSSIA

JULIE POOLE · *Bright Specimen: Poems from the Texas Herbarium* · USA

C.F. RAMUZ · *Jean-Luc Persecuted*
translated by Olivia Baes · SWITZERLAND

MANON STEFAN ROS · *The Blue Book of Nebo* · WALES

ETHAN RUTHERFORD · *Farthest South & Other Stories* · USA

TATIANA RYCKMAN · *The Ancestry of Objects* · USA

MUSTAFA STITOU · *Two Half Faces*
translated by David Colmer · NETHERLANDS

BOB TRAMMELL · *The Origins of the Avant-Garde in Dallas & Other Stories* · USA